Getting Started with Hobby Quad

By Craig S. Issod © 2013-2014 (Updated 05/14)

The Author Trying to "take off" in various ways...

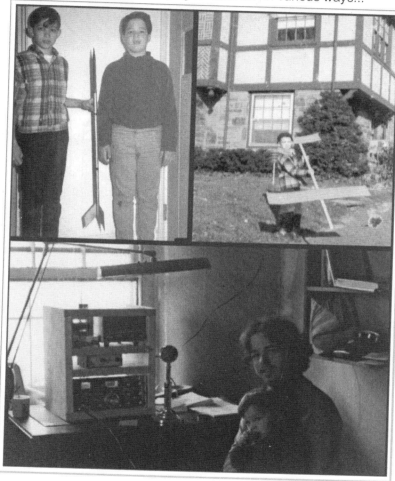

About the Author

By any method necessary, Craig has been attempting to leave the confines of Mother Earth since childhood. In his adult life, he first tried CB Radio with pirate channels, then Ham Radio and vast antenna arrays on his rooftop. Finally he found the promised land of Compuserve (1986), AOL (1988) and the Internet (1994).

Along the way, he developed and sold various alternative energy products, wrote technical manuals, obtained two patents and, along with his spouse of 40+ years, had three children. Craig founded the popular alternative energy web site Hearth.com and a newer hobby site, Droneflyers.com, which is the impetus for this ebook. He won't be happy until drones do some actual work for him and the rest of us.

What others are saying about this book (from Amazon Reviews)

"This book saved me over $200 that I would have spent purchasing the wrong Quad Copter. I highly recommend this book for anyone considering their first experience with Quads"

"Thanks for taking the time and putting this together. Very informative. Clear and concise advice and instruction. Easy for beginners to grasp and understand"

"THIS is what should be included in the owners manual! There is LOTS of useful info on how to repair and troubleshoot."

"Good book, informative, well written, and very helpful for the newbie. What more can I say. A must for those new to flying RC Quads."

Subjects Covered in this Guide

Introduction

What's it all about? - Why would YOU want to fly a Drone? - Use of Terms and Basic Definitions

Basics of Operation

It's Electric! - Aerodynamics of Quadcopters - Like a Human (or robot) - A Short History of Unmanned Flight

Buying a Quadcopter

Choose your Interest - Micros v. Minis v. Full Size - Starting with Simulators - What is this Hobby going to cost? - Which exact model to buy first? - About Returns and Refunds - Your Flying Grounds - Brand Names and Models - What about the Parrot AR Drone ? - 3-Axis vs. 6-Axis Stability - Spare Parts

Flying a Quadcopter

Preparing to Fly - Becoming Familiar with your Transmitter - Booting up your Drone - Testing your Quadcopter - tech info for pilots and nerds - The Next Steps - Landing your Drone - first modifications - Trimming your Quadcopter - Flying Patterns - Do you have the "Right Stuff"? - More Tips for Beginners - Graduation Day

More Information

DIY Drone Repair and Upkeep - Tools of the Trade - A Primer on Aerial Photography and Video - Programmable R/C Transmitters

Your Next Quad

Choices - Larger Quads are more modular - Telemetry - The AR Drone - DJI Phantom - Aerial Photography and FPV - Flight Controllers - A Short Course on Drone Batteries

Appendix

Safety Warnings - Drone Troubleshooting - Glossary - 10 Models to consider for 2014 - Links - List of Manufacturers

Introduction

The last couple of years brought an explosion in news reports regarding drones and other unmanned aerial vehicles. Although many of these reports focus on the well-known military models (Predator, Skyhawk, etc.), the bigger news is the progress in aerial robotic machines which can do a number of tasks - from crop inspection to search and rescue to photography and video. Our beginners guide will focus on consumer and hobby drones - those which you and I can buy and fly on a budget.

What's it all about?

They go by many names - Quadcopters, Quadrotors, Personal Drones, Multirotors, UAV's and even "toys", but these amazing flying machines contain advanced technology and are about to transform our world and our lives in many ways. What's more, you and I and others who are hobbyists, photographers, pilots or just have interest in technology can participate in this revolution at a very low cost.

Where are we now and where are we headed?

2012 and 2013 saw explosive growth in the market and technology, as costs have gone down and capabilities have gone up. In 2014 this is continuing. These leaps forward were driven by lower prices for the important electronic components, which was in turn driven by the rise of hundreds of millions of smartphones and game machines! The same electronic components which power our phones and game consoles (accelerometers, gyroscopes, GPS) help keep a drone flying. Cameras are also getting smaller and less costly, again driven by the market for millions of them inside smartphones, tablets and computers.

Why fly a Drone?

Drones have advanced greatly over the last couple of years - but what's in it for you? Here are just a few of the reasons you may want to take up this pursuit:

Aerial Photography and video -
how would you like a picture of your house, the local valley and farms, the beach or your park from high above? Your drone allows you take pictures and videos as in the photograph below.

Image from 300 foot height using $100 quadcopter (WL v262) and $80 Camera

Another popular type of video is called FPV or First Person View. In this case, the drone has a camera which beams video back to a set of video goggles or a screen. This allow the operator to feel the sensation of flying and twisting through trees, down a path or over a stream.

Racing, Flips and Acrobatic Moves

Some flyers have the competitive spirit and like to push things to the limit. You can learn a number of fancy moves to impress yourself and your friends! Others enjoy the social aspect of hobbies. There are even meets where you can fly your quadcopter in races, demonstrations or just for camaraderie.

Technical Aspects, Modification and Building

Do you enjoy technology, engineering, futuristic pursuits, inventing and expanding your general knowledge? This hobby will allow you to satisfy any level of these interests. Beginners might feel a sense of accomplishment by replacing a few small parts while others build their own quadcopters using custom parts - many of which they make or modify themselves. Others write and modify programs which improve the stability and other aspects of flight control. If you are part of the new "Maker" movement, you'll find many ways to improve these machines.

Fun and Stress Relief

You will often find yourself laughing out loud as well as forgetting about all the troubles of the world as you build, fly or fix your personal drone.

Future Commercial and Non-Profit Uses

There are numerous potential applications of drone technology for the advancement of mankind. These range from search and rescue to mapping to crop inspection and spraying. Potential uses are only limited by your imagination. As with any such venture you need to start with a basic knowledge foundation, which is the intent of this book.

Parrot AR Drone Quadcopter - note the 4 propellers

When you are finished reading it, you should know more about the subject of drones than most of your peers and therefore be able to help others. Even better, you will be able to actually buy and fly drones successfully!

Use of Terms and Basic Definitions

Throughout this booklet, we will use the term "drone", "quad" and "quadcopter" interchangeably, drone being the common use of the news media while quadcopter is more descriptive of the current crop of consumer models. Not all drones are quadcopters. A more accurate name might be UAVs, which stands for "unmanned aerial vehicles". Some use the term "robotic" or "autonomous" in their descriptions, indicating the drone may have more advanced capabilities, such as flying a pre-programmed flight path without operator input or control.

Since this is a Newbies Guide, we will start with only a few definitions - a more complete glossary is at the end of the book.

Drone - a catch-all term used to describe any or all unmanned aerial vehicles.

Quadcopter (quad)- an aerial vehicle which uses four (4) propellers that provide all the lift and steering functions. Similar names are assigned to designs with 3-10 arms and propellers (tricopter, hexacopter, octocopter, multirotor, etc.)

Autonomous - not subject to control from outside, often used to describe a drone which follows a preset path using GPS or other means, as opposed to being actively steered by radio control.

For ease of description, most of our pictures and examples will use quadcopter or quad as the subject.

Basics of Operation

It's Electric!

Why are the new vehicles so different than the former toy helicopters and planes? In a nutshell, it comes down to vast improvements in batteries, hardware and in flight control software programs. The new breed of LiPo batteries (lithium polymer) have a higher power to weight ratio, meaning they can power heavier devices and keep them in the air longer. The same batteries also power the electronics and cameras your quadcopter will use.

The current crop of batteries are capable of keeping quadcopters aloft for periods from 5 to 25 minutes, quite an accomplishment when you consider some of these machines can travel well over a mile in that time. More advances are assured in the future, so specifications will improve.

A quadcopter uses four propellers, two of them rotating clockwise and two counterclockwise. This creates a balanced effect, so that the quadcopter can hover with reasonable stability. The following diagrams and descriptions will help the newbie understand how the brains and brawn of these machines work in tandem to provide the magic of unmanned flight.

Aerodynamics of Quadcopters

Truth is they have no real aerodynamics! These are basically motors and propellers that can only fly with the help of their computer brains. Unlike a plane or even a regular helicopter, failure of an engine or part will invoke gravity without any glide ratio at all. Hobbyists have therefore been able to build quadcopters out of tupperware boxes (for landing in water), foam boards ($5 in frame costs), plastic wheels and other such materials.
It does help for quadcopters to be slightly streamlined as wind will not have as much of an effect on them.

Like a Human (or robot)

It may help to consider the quadcopter as a robot, with the basic internal functions attempting to mimic those of your own body. The first step in movement is your eyes, ears and other senses gathering input or instructions from the environment around you. With a quadcopter, this would be the instructions being given to the drone by the pilot or by a set of pre-programmed steps. In most cases the operator will be actively giving instructions to the flying quadcopter through the use of a radio control transmitter or a smartphone/tablet. You will notice that many discussions of quadcopters use the term "R/C" in them - which means "Radio Controlled".

Item #1 below is the transmitter (TX), usually handheld, which is beaming the instructions to the drone. The part labeled #2 is the receiver - this is also a radio part and it's function is to talk to your transmitter and hand over the instructions to item #3, the Flight Controller, which sends power to #4, the motors.

The flight controller (F/C) is the CPU (central processing unit) or brain of the quadcopter. Like a human brain, it has pathways for information both in and out. Here are the main inputs:

1. Power from the batteries
2. Instructions from your transmitter (usually in your hands).
3. Status reports from a number of tiny instruments built into the quadcopter

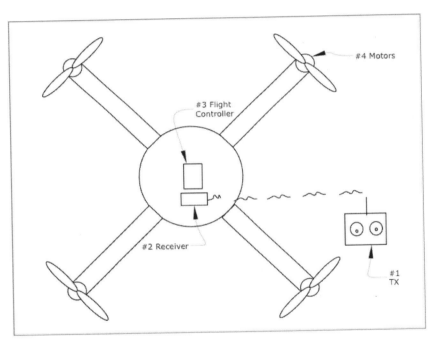

main circuit board. These include gyroscopes for leveling, accelerometers to measure speed and direction, barometers and sonar for height control and GPS and compasses for determining your position on the earth. Simple quadcopters may only have gyroscopes, while very advanced models will have many or all of the above.

Based on the combination of all these inputs, the Flight Controller (FC) makes decisions, most importantly exactly how much electrical power to apply to each of the four motors (#4 in the picture).

As an example, if you desire to fly forward, that requires the quadcopter to tilt in that direction - you should be familiar with this type of flight by having watched helicopters. By tiling forward, the propellers act to keep the vehicle in the air and to propel it forward simultaneously. In the case of a quadcopter, the command to move forward will put less power to the front two motors and more to the rear two, resulting in the machine leaning forward and being propelled in that direction. Side to side movement is accomplished in much the same way - the FC "brain" eases up on two propellers and powers the opposite two slightly stronger.

The comparison with your body is that the flight controller is the brain, the wires are the blood vessels and nerves, and the motors are your muscles, limbs and hands. Like your body, each system constantly gives feedback to the brain, resulting in amazing capabilities of movement.

A Short History of Unmanned Hobbyist Flight

The first demo of a Radio Controlled vehicle was in 1898, when N. Tesla showed a working R/C boat at an electrical expo at Madison Square Garden. He claimed the boat had a "borrowed mind" and obtained U.S. patent number 613,809 for various R/C schemes.

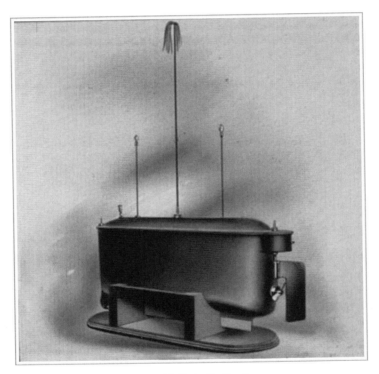

Tesla's R/C Robotic Boat

Some hobbyists may remember building balsa wood airplanes many years ago. In fact, they remain quite popular today. It often took months to build these planes and the final results were quite impressive, but extremely fragile. Many were never flown - the completed plane with paint and decals graced many a man cave. Others installed small gas engines to drive the propellers and ran the planes in a circle, tethered to the ground with a rope. More daring hobbyists set up the planes so they would fly circles and land when they ran out of gas. Suffice it to say that one crash or bad landing often destroyed hundreds of hours of hard and meticulous work.

By the 1960's, radio controlled wing surfaces and rudders were allowing better control of the aircraft and the invention of the transistor meant that radio and other electronic components could be made much smaller and lighter. At the same time, another method of flight became quite popular - model rocketry. These were quite sophisticated and able to travel thousands of feet into the sky. Some of the models featured one-shot film cameras, which provided a great addition to the hobby. Other carried payloads, including small animals. In fact, your friendly author has sent mice up 1,000 feet or more in padded capsules, with all returning safely to earth by parachute.

As mentioned earlier, it is the coming together of all the various electronic and electric technologies, from batteries to radios, which now allows for much more advanced vehicles. Just as importantly, advances in materials such as foam, carbon fiber and fiberglass have allowed for aerial vehicles which last more than a few flights. Some quadcopters can drop out of the sky from 100 feet and suffer little or no damage!

Whereas early models required various skills and determination to build, fix and operate, some current models can be purchased, used and enjoyed by almost anyone - with some caveats (more on that later).

Buying a Quadcopter

Choose your Interest

As with any pursuit, consider what your particular interest is and how you would like to proceed in the hobby. Some examples follow:

Stress relief - Flying a quadcopter engages you fully and, like sailing or many other activities, you will find all other thoughts have left your mind...a good thing, in most cases!

Photography/Video - Quadcopters and other drones are getting advanced enough to do some very decent imagery work! These advances will continue. By learning now, you will be in a better position to take advantage of new advances as they hit the market.

Technology/Learning - there is a LOT to learn if technology and the mechanics of flight interest you. You can delve deeply into customization, building your own quads and polishing you your soldering and innovation skills.

Whatever your reasoning, most newbies should start at the same place - with the purchase of micro or mini sized quadcopter (and/or a good simulator) and hours of initial practice.

First Newbie Rule of Drones

You WILL crash your quadcopter many times while you are learning and repairs/replacements for a small quad are much less expensive than with a larger model.

Micros vs. Minis vs. Full Size

Although there is no official definition of these size ranges, a rough grouping would go somewhat like this:

Micro drones/quadcopters - these fit into the palm of your hand and measure 3 to 4 inches diagonally motor to motor. Most of them are "direct drive", which means the motors directly spin the propellers (no gears). Total weight is approx. 1.5-2.5 ounces (40-60 grams) with battery. A new breed called "nano's", smaller than micros, has recently hit the scene.

Mini drones/quadcopters - these are quite a bit larger and measure 8-10" diagonally motor to motor. Many of them use the same motors as the Micros, but use gearing to drive larger propellers. Total weight is usually approx. 3 ounces (80+- grams) with battery.

Full Size Quadcopters - are classified by weight rather than size, as the bigger motors and batteries and payloads are the most important parts of the system. Most larger quads are direct drive - that is, the motors directly mount to the propellers. They weigh in as "heavyweights" at between 1 to 2.2 lb+ (1/2 to 1+ kg) You don't even want to think about what will happen if one of those fall on you or hit your car!

For newbies, either a micro or a mini will be a fine learning platform. Those who intend to learn indoors will probably be better off with the micro size, however the nano's can be too small for some (harder on the eyes and have tiny controllers, etc.)

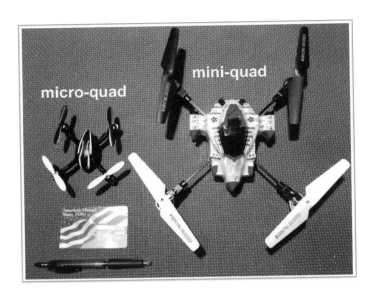

Starting with Simulators

There are computer programs available which may help give you the feel of flying a quadcopter. These run the gamut from inexpensive smartphone or tablet apps to much more sophisticated PC and Mac software which can use a real R/C transmitter connected to your computer via USB. Some examples of the genre and their capabilities are as follows:

> Heli-X (www.heli-x.net) - This is a program which has numerous models of quadcopters built into it. A program such as this can really help you to learn to fly - and, although somewhat costly ($70-$180), are definitely worth the money for the serious pilot who wants to crash less in the real world. Note - a free trial is available, so be sure it works and suits your style before you make a purchase.

> ARDrone Sim - This is an ipad/android app which simulates the AR Drone model quadcopter. It does not have the level of sophistication that the full-fledged programs do, but will give the beginner some idea

of how these machines work. It sells for about $2, so is probably a good purchase for any beginner who wants a short experience of the AR Drone. Speaking of Budget.....

IndoorHeliSim - a free android app that is quadcopter only. This app simple, but effective and had various settings so you can get the feel as a beginner or a more advanced flyer.

How much money will this hobby cost?

This is somewhat variable depending on your wants, needs and budget. If you are happy with the smaller range of quadcopters, a year of fun can be had for the price of a couple fancy dinners out. On the other hand, if you are the proverbial fool who is easily parted with his/her money and buy a $1,000+ setup and instantly dunk it in the river while taking your first video (yes, it's been done), then it will set you back quite a bit more. Since this is a newbies book, let's set a first year budget of about $400 total for a couple small quads, extra batteries, accessories, modifications and repairs. If you decide to take a step up to much larger craft like an AR Drone, Phantom 1 or Blade 350qx the total will likely be double that or more.

Which model to buy first?

As in many other endeavors, not only is the brand and model of importance, but also the vendor (store, online site) you decide to purchase from. Many vendors are China or Hong Kong based and some offer very good prices and are reliable and honest. However, a (USA-based) newbie should consider purchasing from a US based vendor (shipper) when possible for a number of reasons. First, communication with the foreign vendors can often be difficult - not so with your local hobby shop or the better US based sellers. Secondly, it can take weeks for shipments to arrive - no need to play the waiting game to save $5 or $10.

Consider the return policy (defective product), parts availability and advice. Therefore, the author suggests one of the following vendors or types of vendors:

A local hobby shop - Unfortunately, many areas do not have shops that specializes in quadcopters - but, if you do, this may be the first place to look. Check to see if they have a friendly and knowledgeable staff and can answer your questions and concerns.

Online specialists or Big Retailers - there are a number of small vendors that specialize in quadcopters. Some examples at the time of this writing:

MassiveRC - A florida based small business offering micros and minis along with parts and good service.

Horizon Hobby - maker and distributor of the well regarded Blade products - known for good support after the sale.

Amazon and eBay also have nice selections - often sold through retailers who partner with them.

Quadcopters are popular all over the world. In fact, sales of this book are doing very well in the UK, France as well as elsewhere. Many people have no choice but to purchase from the Hong Kong and Chinese vendors - and there are some with very decent reputations. As of this writing, Banggood.com is one such vendor which seems to treat customers well. As always, check into the reputation of your chosen vendor. It will be easy to find discussions about the various suppliers on the online R/C forums.

About returns and refunds

It is rare for a new quadcopter to have factory defects - more likely, the customer takes it out the box, flies it into a couple walls and then claims it's broken. In other cases, the customer simply does not know how to calibrate or fly the drone. Most vendors do not accept returns of used quadcopters - as well they shouldn't - since most damage is of the "you crashed it, you broke it" variety. However, for those cases where something is truly wrong out-of-the-box, the return policies of Amazon and other vendors (and even paypal payment) could come in handy. Using the Chinese vendors, very popular due to low pricing, usually means that you cannot return the product even if defective in the box. Depending on the vendor, you may be able to get a replacement part for no charge.

Your Flying Grounds

Before choosing a model and size, consider your living and yard spaces and where you intend to do most of your learning. If you picked this book up mid-winter in Maine, chances are that you are going to try to learn indoors! The same goes if you live in a small apartment - a micro quad will make a smaller space seem a little bit bigger, so they can be ideal for those who are a bit tight on space. Some other considerations to keep in mind are:

1. Wind resistance - micros, since they provide a smaller wind profile, are usually better in a breeze.

2. Visibility - as you improve you may have interest in flying your quad a bit further away from your person - a micro will quickly become a very small dot once it is more than about 40 feet away! Minis can be flown up to 200 feet away with some success.

Most flyers will eventually have at least one of both sizes, so you really can't go wrong with this decision.

Note - although learning indoors is possible, your family is unlikely to take to you crashing into the good furniture. An open basement or garage provides a better starting place - even better would be to have a practice room with carpet or soft flooring!

Brand Names and Models

The following units are examples of good first quads.

Hubsan X4 -H107 (Micro - $50-$65) - buy the optional prop guard if you are just getting started. This is an improved newer version of the X4...the first version had some shortcomings. A similar sized model from another maker with a bit more manners is called the JXD 388 Aerocraft (no prop guards available on this model)

Blade Nano QX (Micro - $90) - if you don't mind spending the money, this is a very high quality and capable learning machine. It is nano-sized, so mostly for smaller indoor rooms.

Syma X1 or X3 (Mini - $30-$45) - these can be ideal first quads for those on a budget who want to learn how to manually fly a quadcopter - the X3 has integrated propeller guards.

WL Toys V202/212 (Micro - $55) - two great machines, the 212 being a slightly newer and more advanced design.

These, of course, are not the only quadcopters which would fit a beginner, but they should give most fledgling pilots a good place to start. The appendix contains both a list of manufacturers and a list of some of the quadcopters to consider in 2014. You can also find up-to-date reviews at Droneflyers.com

<- - Hubsan X4 with Prop Guards

What about the Parrot AR Drone ?

The AR Drone is a mid-sized drone which is controlled from a smartphone or tablet computer. This is an machine with a full feature set - however it operates differently than most of the quadcopters on the market. A informational chapter on the AR Drone is located later in this book. Read the AR section and also "The Right Stuff" to determine if an AR may fit your needs. In most cases, beginners would be much better off starting with lower priced and smaller quads to build up some "stick time".

3-Axis vs. 6-Axis Stability

Another consideration when choosing a first quadcopter is whether you want to learn in a more manual fashion or have " helpers" in the form of features which make flying and control easier. Although these terms sound very technical, the summary is that 6-axis quadcopters will self-level when the operator takes their fingers off the right control stick. 3 (or 4) axis models will continue in the direction they were going - even if that direction is a steep angle toward the ground. In general, a 6 axis quad will be easier to fly, but that may not be what you desire. As an example, if your interest in this hobby involves flying acrobatically, doing flips, racing pylons, etc. then you will need a lot of manual skills. The 3 or 4 Axis quad will force you to learn more about all the forces in motion. If you really want to learn some of the ropes, consider the 3-4 axis a better tool for the job - or, get one of each! One will build your confidence and the other will build your skill set. At the time of this writing, these are some popular starter quads and their number of axis:

3 or 4 Axis - Syma X1 X3, WL Toys 929, HCW 553

6 Axis - Blade Nano QX, Walkera QR Ladybird, WL Toys V202/212/222, Vitality H36, MJX X100, Hubsan X4 H107, JXD 388

(Before buying, confirm the above information with other users and the vendor.)

Certain models, such as many in the Blade line, have two modes - so-called "Safe" mode which is 6-axis as well as a more manual mode.

Whether 3,4 or 6 axis, start with a model which you know is a good one for beginners. Use online reviews at Amazon or the advice of a good vendor for your final selection. Or, join our forums at droneflyers.com/talk and ask away!

Spare Parts

It's best to buy a small supply of replacement parts along with your quadcopter - this will help you avoid disappointment when your propellers crack or your sole battery runs out! If possible, ask your supplier what parts they would suggest for a beginner. Examples include:

1. Purchase at least one or two additional batteries. Each battery will provide up to 10 minutes of flight time, but could take up to one hour to recharge.

2. Propellers - many of the kits come with a set of extra props - but some of the micros can go through them fairly quickly. You may want to order another couple sets.

3. Motors - it is likely that you will destroy a motor or two in the first few weeks of use. It does take good eyesight and some basic mechanical ability (some require solder, others plugs) to replace a motor on these quads. If you have what it takes, then order one of each (clockwise and CCW) motors or complete motor/arm assemblies.

If you find that parts are not easily available, it may be good to change your purchasing decision to a model where the vendors have plenty of spares. You don't want the lack of a $4 part to keep you grounded. Some quadcopters are so inexpensive that you can buy two - one to fly and one for spares, and still spend only $80 or so in total.

Quadcopters also differ in how easy they are to repair (see section "DIY Drone Repair and Upkeep" later in this book). Many require basic soldering skills as well as nimble fingers and good eyesight to make a repair. Others may have plug-in motors which are more modular and easier to replace.

Flying a Quadcopter

Preparing to Fly

It's an exciting day!

Your new quadcopter is unpacked and sitting on the table in front of you. The first order of business is going to be to charge up the batteries. Most of the low cost drones come with a USB cable that connects to the battery and provides the charge. Some come with a plug-in AC charger. Either way, get your batteries charged up ASAP so you can get your quad up and running.

Your transmitter needs a couple batteries also - usually AA. Make sure you have these on hand.

While your batteries are charging, scan your owners manual as well as any online reviews of your quad model. Many of the manuals are quite poor in their translation from Chinese to English, so don't expect to understand every word. Luckily for you, most of the mini and micro quads will work fine without much initial tuning.

Note: LiPo batteries should be charged on a fireproof surface - it is remotely possible for them to self ignite! Keep them away from loose papers, etc. and charge inside an ash tray, small bowl or similar container. PLEASE READ OUR SAFETY APPENDIX BEFORE CHARGING OR FLYING YOUR QUADCOPTER.

Becoming Familiar with your Transmitter

Most quads are sold with a transmitter which is set up as "mode 2". This means that the throttle is on the left while the right stick controls the pitch and roll (forward/backward and left/right) of the drone. A typical TX panel is shown below:

Typical Mode 2 (Left Throttle) Transmitter Layout

The left stick controls the speed of the propellers and therefore is set all the way back (down) before flying. The right stick should be centered for testing and most liftoffs. The small silver switches, two under the sticks and two toward the center, are for "trimming" the quadcopter so it hovers without drifting off to one angle or another.

Booting up your Drone

Caution - the spinning propellers on ALL quadcopters could cut or injure humans or pets! We'll discuss safety in more detail as we go along, but please take basic common sense precautions when using your new quadcopter and charging your LiPo batteries. Most importantly, avoid any situation where people or pets could come into contact with your operating quadcopter.

Read your owners manual for full instructions on your particular models - here are the usual steps involved in booting a mini or micro drone.

1. Have transmitter ready - and powered with the specified batteries (usually AA). Make certain that the throttle (left stick) is off (down fully toward you).

2. Insert quadcopter LiPo battery into quadcopter frame as shown in manual.

3. Connect battery leads - note, some batteries auto-connect when you insert them.

4. Immediately set the quad down on a flat and level surface. This step is especially important as many quads use their initial position as a reference for how straight and level they will fly. (certain newer models may not require this flat surface)

5. Turn on the transmitter - most will go through a series of beeps and then stop beeping. This indicates the transmitter is "bound" to your quadcopter. It is often necessary to move your throttle stick forward and backward slightly to "arm" your quadcopter. Certain models require other action to arm - this will be detailed in your owners manual.

That's it! Your quadcopter is ready to fly - but are you? Probably not, so let's go through a series of short checks so we don't run into many surprises.

Testing your Quadcopter

The first-time pilot should continue slowly so that their craft (or the family cat) is not destroyed too quickly. One testing technique involves weighting the quad down so it does not fly and then slowly checking all the transmitter functions. Here are a series of steps to do so:

1. Place a small weight, such as a wrench, etc. so that it holds your quad down (near the center!) without being near the spinning propellers. Depending on the particular model, you may have to use a small piece of string, wire or a rubber band to hold the weight to the center of the quad

2. STAND BEHIND THE QUADCOPTER FACING IN THE SAME DIRECTION AS IT'S NOSE. Slowly apply power to the propellers by pushing the left stick (throttle) forward. The propellers should spin up and increase in speed as you push the throttle up. Do not push the stick all the way forward, just enough to start getting the feel of the controls.

3. Once you are comfortable with the spinning props, test the basic functions of the right stick on your transmitter. This stick is normally centered - pushing forward on it should make the drone lean (with the weight on) in the forward direction of flight, while pulling back should do the opposite. Pushing the right stick to the left should make the quad lean left, while pushing it to the right should make it lean right.

If all is well, your quad and you are ready to attempt flight...after a short technical break.

For Pilots, Nerds and other know-it-alls

The various directions in which an aircraft moves have names - as do the usual flight controls which make the vehicle take these actions. The testing phase above describes two axis of movement, those being forward and backwards and left and right. The following definitions will apply:

Pitch - this describes the angle of the quadcopter as relating to level, whether front to back or side to side.

Aileron - this is the flight control used to make the quadcopter lean left or right - the actual movement is called "roll" or "banking".

Elevator - this is the flight control used to make the quad angle up or down when facing forward. Pitch is the term used to describe the effect of the elevator on the nose of the aerial vehicle.

Rudder - This describes the flight control which makes the quad rotate on it's center axis - that is, stay level and spin (as in dance pirouettes!)

Since a quadcopter is computer controlled, they don't have the actual flaps as with a fixed wing aircraft - but if they did, the Elevators would be the tail flaps and the ailerons the wing control surfaces. Instead, control is achieved by varying the exact amount of power to each of the rotors.

Whew! I'm glad that's over with - now let's get back to flying.

Lifting off and Hovering

Remove any weights which you may have used to hold your quad to the ground during testing. Ideally, you are outside over grass for your first flights as the inevitable crashes are unlikely to do as much damage.

Next, while standing behind the quadcopter, slowly apply power to the throttle by moving it forward. Continue applying power until your machine lifts off the

Elevator - this Quad is pitching (flying) forward   Aileron - this Quad is banking left

ground. It's best to initially raise the quad 1 to 2 feet off the ground, as they can be quite unstable when very close to floors, walls and ceilings. You want to get it high enough to be in "free air". Ideally, your quad will hover and not move too quickly in any direction. This indicates that your gyro is properly set. However, if you are in a confined area getting the hang of a hover could take some time.

If your quadcopter seems erratic and moves quickly in any direction without your steering it, you should land it, disconnect the battery, and then reconnect it - making 100% certain that you are on a perfectly level surface. Then try again - you should not attempt to fly until you can hover within a small area - say about 6 X 6 feet. This may require small amounts of stick input from your right stick. If you are, as instructed, standing behind your quadcopter, the right stick should steer the quad as shown below.

The left stick is the throttle AND, when moved left and right rotates the craft on it's axis.

Depending on your level of coordination and previous experience with similar types of controls, it may take quite a few attempts before you are able to hover properly. Most of your early flights will be taking off and then landing quickly when you feel the quad is out of control. Don't fret - practice makes perfect and you will succeed after enough attempts. Take baby steps because attempts to fly far and fast will definitely result in losing or destroying your quadcopter.

Note: We have made a number of videos and other aids to go with this booklet which you can find on our blog & forum at droneflyers.com

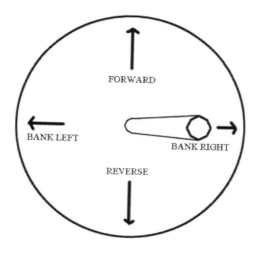

The Next Steps

Once you can successfully hover, it's time to fly further away from the nest! This will familiarize you with the way your quadcopter responds to movement of your control sticks. The more room you have, the better - a area at least 50ft square should do nicely for micro and mini quads. Your first exercise should be to fly your quad directly away from you - forward - by pushing the right stick slightly forward. Of course, you also have to keep the perfect amount of pressure on the left throttle stick - quadcopter flying is multitasking! Fly 10-20 feet forward and then pull slowly back on the right stick to bring the quad back toward you. As with hovering, this may take you some time to master - but don't give up! It's all a matter of training your brain and reflexes - not much different than driving a car, which would be impossible if you hadn't put in so many hours of repetition.

Landing your Drone

Unless you have an AR Drone or other model with automatic landing, you are going to have to learn the technique of landing. One way or another, each takeoff means one landing - although some are what we call "unscheduled landings" (crashes). Landing can be harder than it seems, especially on 3-axis craft which must be perfectly level in order to avoid the propellers hitting the ground before the landing gear touches. Practice on a soft surface such as short-cut grass or carpet. Lift your quad a few feet off the ground and gain control so that you hover under control - then slowly back down on the throttle until the drone nears the ground.

It's VERY important to cut the throttle 100% during crash or hard landings, as keeping power to the blades and motors when they strike grass or the ground will harm them. Most of the suggested quadcopters can drop from a few feet up (or even higher!) to a soft surface with absolutely no damage - unless you keep the throttle on!

Your First Modification - may be landing gear!

Now that you are learning how to fly, you may notice that your drone has certain shortcomings. Some units have props and gears very close to the ground so that landing and taking off on grass can become difficult. One of the joys of this hobby is making small improvements in and personalizing your drone...your first chance at improvement may be to install a softer or higher landing gear. Depending on the size and weight of the quad, you may use small pieces of foam, lightweight balls or cable/zip ties. The zip ties can be mounted in various ways as shown in the pictures below. Soft or springy landing gear provides the additional benefit of allowing for harder landings on blacktop or cement without damage to your quad.

**Zip Tie
Landing Gear**

Continue to practice your landings until you are very confident that you can place your craft where you want it. Set up "landing pads" around your practice area and try to land on the target. Then, as you hone your skills, try to land in the center of the target.

Trimming your Quadcopter

If your quadcopter seems to drift in the same direction constantly, you may need to trim your transmitter slightly. Most transmitters have four switches which can be nudged in one direction or the other to help the quad hover in a more centered fashion. An an example, if the quadcopter tends to drift forward, the two middle switches could be pressed down a few clicks to favor the opposite direction. Note: do not use trim unless you are 100% sure that the quadcopter has been initialized (started) on a flat and level surface. Trim is only for making very small adjustments - if your drone is heading very quickly in one or another direction, it is likely the problem is elsewhere.

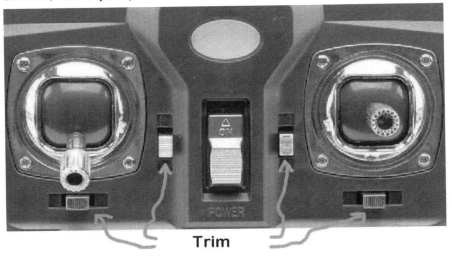

Trim

Flying Patterns

Once you master taking off, hovering, landing and basic forward and backward flight, it's time to combine some of your moves. Watch some of the youtube videos on quadcopters and you will see experienced users doing banked turns and figure 8's. It takes many hours of practice to master these turns and it won't happen if you are worried about crashing an expensive drone! Use a micro or mini drone- outside over grass if possible - and it won't matter how many times your machine hits the deck. Dust it off and try again.

Do you have the "Right Stuff"?

At some point it may become evident that the Air Force would probably not pick you as a candidate for Top Gun flight school. Don't fret - all is not lost! If you find that manual flying is too difficult for you to master, you still have many options to enjoy the quadcopter hobby and pursuit. Many of the newer (and future) quadcopters have stabilization features and some can even be programmed for autonomous flight - that means they will take off, fly around a field by themselves, and then land within a few yards of their takeoff point!

The main thing to keep in mind, if you (like me) are all thumbs, is to research and buy the proper machines for your capabilities and needs. Models such as the DJI Phantom, Blade 350 QX and AR Drone have loads of intelligence programmed into them. More advanced models take some, but not all, of the piloting load off the operator.

More Tips for Beginners

Some of these tips are mentioned in the text, but here they are in one place so you can print them out and paste them above your hobby bench or desk!

1. Charge your batteries correctly - Buy and use a better battery charger than the USB-direct model which comes with your first quad. Do not overcharge or over-drain your batteries and they will last much longer.

2. Plug in your quadcopter while it is on level ground and leave it level for about 10-12 seconds. Most quads use their initial position to determine what "level" is.

3. Make certain that your Transmitter throttle (usually the left stick) is in the down position when plugging in your drone. Do not transport or handle your quadcopter with the transmitter still in your hands as you will likely hit the throttle and perhaps cut your fingers, etc. It is best to turn the TX off or disconnect the battery if moving the quad from place to place.

4. Don't be tempted initially to "see what my quad can do". Doing so will almost surely cause loss or crashing of your quad. Wait until you have some hours on the stick before venturing too high or far.

5. When a crash is inevitable - OR, when landing, immediately turn the throttle down to zero. Most mini and micro quads can take a crash very well - but if the throttle is not turned down fully when you crash, you'll do more damage to the propellers and motors.

AR Drone 2.0 Quadcopter

The AR Drone

In many ways, the Parrot AR Drone, released in 2010, foresaw the current boom in consumer quadcopters. Although there had been an active geek culture building and programming quads prior to that date (2005 on), the AR Drone fired up the fancy of many and was well covered in the press. Brookstone was the initial primary vendor and it was sold as a "flying video game", although I have little idea of what they meant by that! It turned out that the original AR Drone was not quite ready for prime time...lots of problems, including flyaways, inability to control, easily damaged parts, etc. were reported. Customer satisfaction was not high - yet they kept selling and interest remained.

In mid-2012, Parrot released the new AR Drone 2.0 which addressed many of the shortcomings of the 1.0 model and added a higher resolution camera. In 2013, Parrot announced various upgrades to the AR Drone, including a GPS module and longer lasting batteries. Together these may make the AR Drone capable of some autonomous flight (that is, following a series of waypoints you place on google maps, etc.).

AR Drone as a First Quad?

With all these features and a relatively low price, beginners may be enticed to start with this full featured aircraft - however, you keep the following in mind:

6. A beginner cannot reliably fly the AR Drone indoors - the literature may mention it, but anything short of a warehouse is going to feel very small.

7. The AR Drone does not (stock) use a standard R/C Controller, but is instead controlled by smartphone or tablet computer. This generally means shorter range and that the hours you spend learning and flying an AR Drone will not help you as much if you later switch to a standard R/C type transmitter.

8. Parts for the AR Drone (and larger quadcopters in general) are more expensive - meaning if you crash often and hard (and you WILL crash), it will cost you more to repair than a mini or micro.

AR Drone as 2nd or 3rd Quad?

Maybe! The real key with quadcopters is to get enough experience under your belt to truly know what you want to do with them! If you are interested in "sport" flying and racings, the AR is not for you. It's specialty is very stable flight in low wind conditions. It also has some advantages such as relatively low replacement parts cost, safer "cutoff" which stops the propellers when they hit anything (including you), etc.

But let's remember - this is a book for beginners, so let's start with a sub-$100 quadcopter while we drool over the pictures, videos and stories about the more advanced craft!

Putting in your Hours

Assuming you have decided to move ahead with your drone education, the most important continuing effort is to get "stick time". This could be on a good simulator program or around your backyard or a local park. Once you get past the initial learning curve, you will find the experience to be fun and a great stress reliever. You will be concentrating on flying and likely not thinking of anything else!

So, how long will it take? This depends on aptitude as well as a number of other factors such as your age, your familiarity with controllers. Video gamers are likely to find themselves taking to the controls easier than those who have never messed around with joysticks. After 5-10 hours (40-80 flights) it should be safe to call yourself a student pilot.

Moving Forward

Once you master the basics you will probably get more of an idea of exactly where you want to go with this pursuit. Are you more interested in taking videos? or on flying fast, doing flips and racing? Or, are you technical and does the idea of building and modifying drones appeal to you? This is a good time to start doing more research regarding the different brands and models and their specific uses. Many budding pilots will be happier if they stick with the Micro and Mini Quadcopters as opposed to working too quickly toward the larger and heavier models. The smaller units will keep the cost of ownership and repair low and allow for more freedom in your flying (smaller quads make your yard or park seem bigger!). In fact, unless you need the payload capabilities of a large drone, you may never want to move upwards in size.

Size Ranges, Models and Costs

Mini and micro quadcopters usually sell for prices from $40 to $100. There are a few premium models which retail for as high as $150-$200. These drones generally weigh in at about 3 ounces. However, the next step up in size tend to be a whopper. Most mid-sized quads weigh in at 1-2 lbs with battery, meaning they are 5 to 10 times the weight of the Minis. It is somewhat of a mystery why the manufacturers don't produce a mid-range (4-12 oz.) line of drones, but as of this writing very little is available in that weight class. As of mid-2014, some new units are available in this mid-sized range. They include the WL v262, the Eye One Extreme, and the Skytec Butterfly.

The cost of upkeep and repair of a quad tends to relate closely to the original price - as a percentage. As an example, a $50 quad which crashes may need a new propeller and boom ($5) and perhaps a new motor ($5), which equals about 20% of the initial purchase price. A larger quadcopter may end up needing $50-$100 worth of parts for the same crash - or for a much lesser crash because larger and heavier quads get damaged more from a crash.
With this in mind, it's important to consider your overall budget before venturing on in the world of larger drones.

DIY Drone Repair and Upkeep

Even if you are all thumbs, there are some simple repairs that will help you get the most bang for the buck from your quadcopters. Here are some of the more common repairs and the basics needed to perform them.

Propeller Replacement - Propellers for small drones are very inexpensive, so you should replace them once they are bent or otherwise out of shape. Smaller quads have propellers which attach in one of two ways - the micros often have friction-fit (push on) props which only require a deft touch and small fingers to remove and replace. Some hobbyists claim that a small drop of a glue such as Elmers helps them stay on better - yet is easily removed when it's time for replacement. Minis generally have a single phillips head screw holding the propeller to the drive shaft. For this and other repairs, your first tool purchase should be a set of tiny screwdrivers.

Motor Replacement - Motor replacement is a common task on small multirotors. Depending on your hobby skills, you may want to research your initial purchase to find out exactly how the motors are replaced on your particular quad of choice. Some are plug-in, while others require that you solder the new motor (motor comes with leads) to the main circuit board. It's often possible to take a shortcut and simply solder the new motor wires to the cutoffs of the old ones. Motor replacement sometimes requires disassembly of the booms (the cross pieces which hold the motors to the main body).

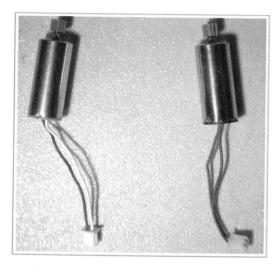

These motors use plugs so no soldering
is required for replacement (WL Toys models)

Boom Replacement

As shown in the photo below, the booms of most Mini quadcopters are press fitted into the main frame and also into the motor pods. The booms are very inexpensive, but you must be careful in your replacement work as it is possible to rip out the motor wires, etc. if you are too rough. If your motors are plug-type, this process is easier - boom replacement on some models will require de-soldering and re-soldering of the motor wires to the main board.

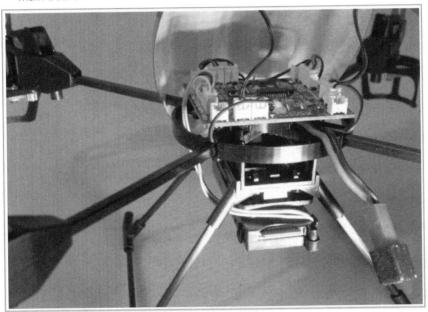

The booms (cross pieces) push into the main round frame - wires run through the boom and are plugged into

Fix it or Sell It?

Other repairs can be done - in fact, you can get virtually any part for most quadcopters, including the main circuit boards. But there comes a time when the repair costs may be adding up. However, don't throw that quad in the trash yet! You can still recoup a decent percentage of your cost by selling it for it's parts content! For example, just your transmitter, which probably never sustained damage, could be worth $20 or so. Add to it some of the parts from your hulk, and you may be able to get $25 or more for what is left of your quadcopter. eBay and RCgroups.com are both places where you could consider selling your parts. Be sure to accurately describe your sale so your buyer and you remain happy after the transaction.

Repair and upkeep is a big part of the enjoyment for many people...but if flying is your only goal, the "use it and then sell it" route may fit your needs. As with all aircraft and mechanical devices, there is a certain cost per hour of operation. This holds true whether you decide to repair...or to replace.

Tools of the Trade

If you enjoy repair and modification, the following tools and supplies should be the beginning of any basic drone tool collection:
1. Razor Blades, X-Acto knives, etc.
2. Electrical tape - various colors can be nice
3. Glue - some superglue as well as perhaps some other glues or epoxy.
4. Mini and micro screwdrivers
5. Soldering Iron with small tip - if you intend to progress further in the hobby, pick up one with interchangeable tips and variable heat. You can find bargain models for about $30 including the tips. Pick up some solder for electronic use (usually rosin-core).
6. Digital Multimeter (voltage meter)

7. Good lighting for the work area as well as a magnifying glass on a stand for inspection of those tiny parts

8. Fastening odds and ends such as velcro, rubber bands and zip ties.

Chances are that some of these items are already sitting around your house or workshop. A nice kit could be put together for less than $50. Look for bargains both online and at the dollar store!

A Primer on Aerial Photography and Video

The idea of taking pictures and videos from aloft is enticing many to join this hobby. It can be tempting to pull out your credit card and buy that top-notch aerial photography platform early in your drone career, but I would caution against it. As mentioned previously, beginners are very likely to crash, lose or otherwise come to a bad end before they get a solid foundation in the basics. Here are some definitions and hints, though, so you can know what the camera carrying options are.

First Person View (FPV) vs. Aerial Photography (AP)

The simplest form of drone aerial photography is accomplished by flying around with a tiny video camera - and retrieving the video from a memory card once the quad has landed. Mini-quadcopters with built in cameras and controls can be found for as little as $80 - however, the resulting pictures and video will not be of a high quality. In order to get higher quality images, you must step up to larger quadcopters as they are capable of greater stability (less wobble) and carrying better cameras. A shortcoming of this method is that you don't see your footage until after you land and download the memory card to a computer.

First Person View (FPV) describes photography where you see what the drone is seeing, or at least a basic preview of it. The video is beamed back to a monitor or to a set of special goggles the operator is wearing. This allows for much more precise control of the scenes being photographed.

Camera types

Aerial cameras often take a beating, so don't want to use a fragile consumer camera for this application. Here are some of the popular cameras and types used in hobbyist (sub-$1,000) Aerial Photography - approx. prices in ():

Included or Optional low-resolution quadcopter camera ($25) - These are included with such models as the well know WL Toys v959 (see Droneflyers.com for full review) and many other models. They are very light in weight and can be turned on and off from the included transmitter.

Keychain Cams ($12-$60) - These are very popular lightweight cameras sold as "keychain spy cameras" which many hobbyists affix to their quadcopters. The more expensive models have a higher resolution and wide angle lenses. The images from these can be very decent if the quadcopter is stable and balanced and the lighting good (bright sunlight is not good for most of these cameras).

Mobius Sport Cam - ($75-$90) - A new entry built specifically for the R/C market, this little wonder provides HD videos, stills (on a timer) and other great features for a low price. It can be lifted by some smaller quadcopters like the WL Toys v262, the new Eye One Extreme, etc.

GoPro and other Sport Cameras ($120-$400) - These are specially made for action - both shockproof and lightweight. Full size quadcopters are required to lift them, while the other models above can be flown from minis and even micros.

The Parrot AR Drone features a built-in front-facing camera which provides medium resolution images and FPV on a tablet or smartphone. It is no doubt the most inexpensive package with all these features, however it comes with limitations such as a shorter range and lack of ability to fly in higher winds. See the chapter on the AR Drone and other information in this book for more detail.

The budding aerial photographer should spend some time on youtube and vimeo looking at various quadcopter videos and the platforms they were taken from. This will give you a good idea of what to expect out of your upcoming purchases.

Please note that true semi-pro aerial photography requires more expensive and heavier quadcopters along with better cameras. Some of the upscale models of drones even fly DLSR's which weigh a couple pounds! Expect such systems to start at about $3,000 and quickly go upwards from there - putting them out of the range of most hobbyists and beginners. The price range of hobby range quadcopters and the associated features are below:

(APV=takes video   FPV=takes video and allow you to see what the quad sees)

$80-$100 - WL Toys V959/V222 - APV only

$200 - Micro and Mini FPV/APV models such as the Hubsan FPV 107D (X4) and other models from Walkera.

$300 - AR Drone by Parrot - FPV and APV - or v262 with Mobius and bargain FPV setup

$700 -$1200+ - Full size quadcopters with GoPro type cameras and APV/FPV system installed.

DIY hobbyists can put together systems in just about any price range from as low as $100. More detail on cameras, FPV and the proper quadcopters to fly them can be found in the section entitled "More on Aerial Photography and FPV" which follows the review of the DJI Phantom later in this book.

Keychain Camera (L) and Mobius HD Camera (R)

Graduation Day

Congratulations! If you've gotten this far you are no longer a complete beginner - in fact, you probably know more about the subject than 98% of the general public! As with any graduation, this is a good time to reflect on both the past and the future. It's also time to make some decisions as to where you want to go in your "drone career". Here are some possible paths to take to drone nirvana:

You enjoy the mini and micro quadcopters and want to continue to pursue this low cost and high value pursuit.

You want to delve further into the hobby in terms of both the technical and learning aspects and the various sizes of quadcopters. You may want to be a full fledged "hacker" and start messing with the quadcopter programming.

You wish to fly larger quadcopters for either photography/video or for flying enjoyment (acrobatics, flips, racing or just messing around), but don't want to delve too deep into the nuts and bolts.

Since this is a newbies book, we won't go too deep into all the technical details, but a basic introduction on how to "step up" follows.

Programmable R/C Transmitters

Advancing in the hobby usually requires at least a basic understanding of the fancier R/C transmitters (TX) which are used with most larger quadcopters. Note the two types shown in the picture following:

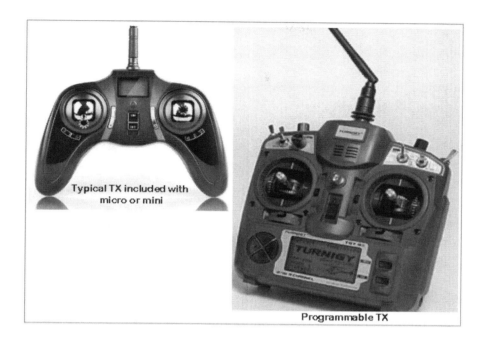

Typical TX included with micro or mini

Programmable TX

The RTF (ready to fly) drones mentioned earlier in this book are sold with a TX which was specially designed and programmed to run only the particular quadcopter it was sold with. However, larger drones are often sold without a TX, so the budding hobbyist will need to learn how to use these.

Fair Warning - you may feel, at first, that you stepped back 20 years and are working with some ancient artifact of the computer revolution. As a rule, they are not user friendly - no color screen, no mice or touch screen, links, help files, or automatic setup wizards. Someday this will change, but for now you will have to join the "club" and slog your way through learning these flight controllers.

The good news is that they are very powerful and flexible. A single model can store the profiles for many flying machines, so if the quad collection builds up you'll only need one or two of these transmitters. They also allow for dialing up-

or-down on the flight characteristics of flying machines, so if you desire your quadcopter to be exceedingly tame, the settings can be changed easily.

R/C transmitters have from 4 to 9+ channels, meaning they can control that many different actions (switches, modes, flight surfaces, etc.) on the model you are flying. The beginning quadcopters mentioned earlier in the book are usually 4 channel - the channels controlling:

Throttle - how much power is being sent to the propellers

Elevators - this makes the quadcopter fly forward or backward by tilting it (pitch)

Ailerons - tilt the copter side to side and... (roll)

Rudder - this makes the quadcopter spin on it's central axis (yaw)

Larger and fancier quadcopters may need more controls, although 5 or 6 channels are enough for most models. Prices range from as little as $50 to as much as $350+, although very decent models can be had for $50-$150. Brands include Turnigy, Walkera, Spektrum, JR, Futaba, FlySky and more.

Your Next Quadcopter

It's time to decide on your next drone - to buy and fly along with a more advanced TX. It's best to start with something small and inexpensive so you learn how the programmable TX works without too much expense. Here are a couple suggestions for your next quad:

One of your existing micro quads? - Some of the mini quads such as the Syma X1, the WL Toys 929,949,959 and others can "bind" to many of the popular programmable transmitters. This means getting the feel of the larger TX and learning about some of the settings while using an inexpensive existing quadcopter.

Q-BOT Micro (also sold as HiSky FF120) - this is a micro quadcopter designed to bind (pair with - and be used with) most transmitters on the market. It sells for less than $50 and has the flight characteristic of a larger quadcopter - highly recommended before you move up to larger models!

Ready to Fly Quads -"The Flip" - If you can't wait before going a bit bigger, this is a quadcopter to consider in the $300 range. It's about $300 and much larger and heavier than the micros or minis. Similar models, both ready to fly and in kit form, are available from various vendors such as multiwiicopter.com.

Some other new entries in the "step up" market include the Blade 350 QX ($400), the Eye One Extreme ($150) and the Walkera QR X350 ($400). The Blade and the Walker feature some GPS modes (return to home automatically) as well as other advanced features.

Larger Drones are more Modular

At the beginning of the book, we covered the basics of how a quadcopter works. However, now that you may be advancing in the hobby, it will benefit you to learn about the various parts and how they function. This will help you both with your shopping and selection and with your troubleshooting.

The following drawing shows a more advanced "modular" quadcopter, which has separate components onboard as opposed to the "all in one" design of the small circuit boards on mini and micro quads. This type of design allows you to select different receivers to mate with your TX - or, to select various brands and types of flight controllers and GPS add-ons.

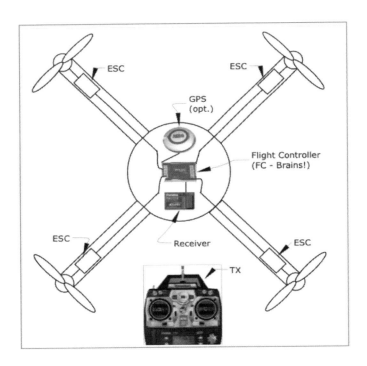

Telemetry - Knowing what is happening aloft

Inexpensive and starter quads are essentially controlled in a one-way fashion - you provide the R/C control and "talk" to the drone, but it doesn't talk back to you. Telemetry is the science of having the vehicle provide real-time data back to you. This ranges from simple things such as the battery level, to more complex data such as wind speed, height above ground, vehicle speed and even the temperature of the motors. This is beamed back to you and shows as a overlay on the quadcopter view (FPV) or on a small display screen of your R/C Transmitter. Telemetry is a very important feature for advanced and more expensive quads, so you will want to educate yourself on the subject as you progress in the hobby.

Understanding the various components will make you a smarter shopper as you will be able to compare the various subsystems by brand name, compatibility, reputation, warranty, etc.

Despite being advertised as such, many larger quads are not sold truly ready to fly - at least not to the consumer of average to low technical ability. There are some exceptions to that rule such as the AR Drone, Blade 350 QX and the DJI Phantom. The later models can be described as major advances in Ready to Fly consumer quadcopters, as they include many advanced features for a relatively low price.

A new article on "Movin on Up" has just been published on the droneflyers.com blog - here is the link: http://droneflyers.com/2014/03/movin-transitioning-toy-class-quad-hobby-grade/

The DJI Phantom - First Mass-Market Consumer Drone?

The DJI Phantom, introduced at the beginning of 2013, represents a major milestone in the adoption of consumer level drones. This is a Quadcopter that, just a few short years ago, would have been impossible to build. Similar vehicles have been built before that time, but they are usually in kit form and require time, patience and mechanical skills. In addition, it is often hit or miss as to how well these homebuilt quads do the job of aerial photography.

The Phantom is sold RTF, or Ready to Fly, complete with transmitter, advanced navigation and software control and the ability to lift high quality cameras for video and still photography. As of this writing (mid-2014), DJI offers at least 4 different models of this quadcopter, some of which come complete with cameras and FPV.

Open the box and you see a quad that LOOKS like a consumer product! No bundles of wires strapped to exposed framing with cable ties, but rather a finished and sleek aerial vehicle that is ready to put into action.

The manufacturer, DJI Innovations, is solidly grounded in this business and is well regarded, making the purchase less of a gamble than a "here today, gone tomorrow" multirotor company. The prices, about $450 (original model), represent a very good value in a mid-sized drone. With the addition of a camera ($50 to $300), you will be ready to take some videos or stills.

The current DJI line appeals to virtually all levels of the multirotor market. While it should not be the first Quad you own, it could easily be the 2nd or 3rd machine you purchase once you learn the basics. The intelligent flight controls should help you avoid many common mistakes and the great videos which DJI has produced on the Phantom's operation should put you into the pilots seat quite quickly.

As always, newer pilots should practice above a soft surface – tall grass, for example, and keep the Quad within a few yards until they understand it's operation. The optional propeller guides are highly recommended for increased safety. Those who buy from a local retail shop may be able to get some lessons from the store personnel or team up with existing owners or a local flying cub for tips and hands-on stick time. DJI has made a series of videos for the Phantom which should be watched by any prospective customer and owner.

All DJI Phantom models have GPS as well as a compass feature. These features can be used in various ways - the TX allows the pilot to turn various functions on or off.

Summary – although not an inexpensive package, the Phantom represents a major step in the world of RTF mid-sized multirotors. Steve Jobs said of the first Apple Macintosh Computers "These are the first computers worthy of criticism". The Phantom fits into the same category and is likely to be the bellwether for what is to come in the future.

UPDATE: We have written an article comparing the 4 currently available DJI models. Please check for the article on our blog at droneflyers.com - the full url is as follows:

Customer Caution: Please check FIRST to see that replacement parts are easily and inexpensively available before buying this or any quadcopter/drone. The best drone isn't any fun when a $12 part is keeping you from flying!

More on Aerial Photography and FPV

Although some larger quads are used for aerobatics, racing and other pursuits, most hobbyists plan for photography to play a role in their more advanced machines. This section will discuss the equipment and costs related to aerial photography.

Earlier in this book we discussed cameras which are available stock on smaller (mini and micro) quadcopters. These cameras are fun learning tools, but have severe limitations when it comes to picture and video quality, range and other issues. Larger and more sophisticated quadcopters will give you more choices in camera, platforms, range and other options.

Payload Capacities and Quadcopter/Camera Size Planning

Stepping up from the mini and micro drones, you'll find quads with larger and more powerful motors and frames as well as much bigger batteries to power them. While most starter quads use 3.7 volt (single cell) LiPo batteries, larger models will often use 2 (7.4v), 3 cell (11.1 volt) or even larger power sources (see section on drone batteries for more info).

As a basic guide to hobby quadcopters, you can expect the following payloads to be lifted with these general categories of quadcopter:

Small multi-cell (batteries) models - 7.4Volt - example models include Hoten-X, WL Toys 262, Eye One Extreme. These can lift in the range of 2 to 4 ounces. (28 to 112 grams).

Mid-Sized Hobby Quadcopters (11.1v) such as the DJI Phantom, Arducopter, Walkera QR X400. These can lift payloads up to 1/2 kilogram (>1 Lb) or more.

Sample Aerial Photographs taken from Quadcopters

High Above Ireland (credit -Gerry Keaveney)

Bogata, Columbia (credit Juan Manuel Ospina)

New England Scene

Rhode Island, USA

Mill Pond and Town, USA

Orchard in Winter, USA

When considering the total weight of cameras, various components must be added up for the true total. These will usually be as follows:

1. Weight of Camera body and lens
2. Weight of fixed and/or moveable mount for camera, including anti-vibration pads, etc.
3. Weight of extra gear such as cables and transmitters for FPV (if desired).

Let's match these payloads up with possible camera/gear combinations. At the lower end, the 2 cell (7.4v) quadcopters can very easily lift the better "keychain" cams which weigh in at 20-40+ grams with mounting. This leaves some payload left for other additions such as ant-vibration mounts or FPV transmitters and cables, which could total as much as another 40 grams. Most quads fly best on less than maximum payload, so try to plan your purchases with extra weight carrying capacity.

Weighing in much heavier will be the GoPro cams as well as similar sports cams - especially if they mounted with their shockproof cases. The older GoPro (Hero2) can weigh 8 oz (1/2 lb or 220+ grams) complete with case and battery. This does not include the FPV cables and transmitters. The next step up in quality cameras are actual consumer digital cameras such as the Sony NEX and/or RX-100 models (approx. 250 grams or 9 oz.) However, it's the brave newbie pilot who would chance flying $700-$1,000 worth of camera when a single crash could destroy it!

Short Discussion of FPV Gear

Most First Person View gear for drones works differently than the purely digital cameras we are used to. These are often analog systems, and therefore use either a different (2nd) camera or an analog A/V output from your existing digital model. This output is coupled to a transmitter with it's own antenna - and often needing it's own battery. The video signal is then transmitted from the quad to your ground station and displayed on a small monitor on on the inside of specially designed googles. Many hobbyists prefer to keep the entire FPV system separate - with it's own small cam. FPV does not require a high resolution, so the camera can be very small and light.

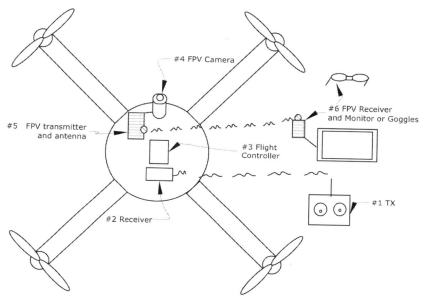

In the diagram above, #4 through 6 are parts of the FPV system. They can be described as:

#4 - FPV Camera or Analog (usually composite) output from existing quadcopter camera (GoPro, Keychain Cam, etc.)

#5 FPV Transmitter and antenna - this takes the "TV Type" signal from the FPV Camera and broadcasts it to the ground.

#6 FPV Receiver and Monitor or Goggles - This receives the signal from your drone and then displays it on a connected monitor or goggles. In some cases, a smart phone or computer tablet acts as both the ground receiver and the monitor.

Some equipment and connections are not shown in the above diagram. These include the battery or power connection to the FPV camera and transmitter and connections for triggering the camera on or off from the ground TX. FPV gear setup can be quite technical - a full discussion is outside the range of this book. If you are not technical, it will probably be best to look for a unit sold RTF (ready to fly) with FPV, such as the Phantom Vision or FC 40. For further reading, see the FPV web sites in the "links" section at the end of this book.

Controlling Photography and Video Cameras Aloft

Simple toy quadcopters such as v959 and v222 have video cameras which can be turned on or off by a button on the transmitter. However, since flight times are fairly short, many users simply turn the video camera on before takeoff and let it run for 6-8 minute duration of the flight. There is a separate control for the snapshot (still picture) function, but such shots are of very poor quality so it may be best just to use a frame from the video for any desired photos.

Larger systems work differently. Ready to Fly FPV systems like the AR Drone and Phantom Vision/FC40 have full control through a wireless connection to a smartphone or tablet, but many quads which carry cameras do not. In these cases, you have a couple choices.

Activate video before quadcopter takes off - again, since the flights are usually short, you can turn on your GoPro or other video camera and let it record the entire flight - then edit it later.

Use Camera with Interval Shooting - many cameras have a setting which is called Interval Shooting or Intervalometer - this allows programmed intervals at which the camera snaps a picture or takes a short video. As an example, a camera can be set to take one picture every 10 seconds for the entire duration of a flight. Only certain cameras have this feature, so check on your choice of cameras to confirm.

Understand Flight Controllers (FC , F/C)

Flight Controllers, as mentioned previously, are the brains of a drone. They are created from a combination of hardware and software, much like modern computers, tablets and smartphones. As you progress in this hobby it may be important to understand the various F/C platforms available to control your drone.

Quadcopter flight controllers are of two basic types:

1. Open Source or Community based projects - these are designs which have been developed and shared and cost nothing to use or modify. The designs consist of both software and hardware. Examples of such projects include:

Openpilot

Ardupilot

Multiwii

KKmulticopter

Although the software code and reference designs are usually free, you still have to buy the actual hardware (circuit boards) as those cost $$ to produce. Upgrading the flight controllers can be accomplished by downloading the newest code and connecting to the flight controller using a USB interface. This is not a task for non-techie beginners.

2. Commercially Developed systems - these are flight controllers developed (or heavily modified from open source) in-house and sold only with a specific model or range of models. Examples include:

Parrot AR Drone FC

Naza (DJI)

Wookong (DJI)

Dualsky (FC450, etc.)

With these flight controllers you are usually tied to the particular manufacturer in terms of upgrades and modifications.

Bare bones flight controllers - selling for as little as $15 - have the ability to manually fly a quadcopter, while more expensive models ($30 - $200+) have advanced capabilities and modular expansion for features such as GPS, Barometers, Sonar, etc. which will help with autonomous (hands-off) flight. Those in the market for more advanced quadcopters should research the various flight controllers and options to make certain that they have the proper functions for their intended use.

A Short Course on Drone Batteries

Most quadcopter batteries are of the LiPo type, which stands for Lithium Polymer. These batteries can store a tremendous amount of energy in a relatively small and light package and are key to modern drone performance. Here are the basics of these batteries.

Your first foray into quadcopters may be with a mini or micro – most of which use a single cell (3.7 volt) LiPo battery and come standard with a USB or plug-in charger. However, once you step up in size to larger and heavier drones, you will find that most of them use batteries which are much larger in size, weight, amperage and voltage. Most LiPo batteries are built of 3.7 volt cells, so they often are a multiple of that number – the most popular for larger quads being 11.1 volt (3 cell) packages.

Ratings are given in maH (milliamp hours) - the higher the number, the more power the battery contains. Micro and Mini quads will carry 200-700 maH batteries, while a typical mid-sized drone may have a 2000-3000 mah rating.

Although the USB and stock chargers may be OK for the small batteries, experienced pilots should invest in a "smart" charger, which not only charges the batteries but monitors their exact voltage and knows when to stop. More advanced chargers are also capable of balancing the battery cells - a function which is needed to properly charge batteries with multiple cells. Lastly, the fancier chargers can be rigged up to charge multiple batteries at once, which can be of great benefit to those who want to get in the air quickly.

"Smart" chargers can be purchased in the range of $20-$45 - although you may need some extra cables and adapters to charge your various batteries. A smart charger should be on the "must have" shopping list for any beginner who wants to advance in the hobby.

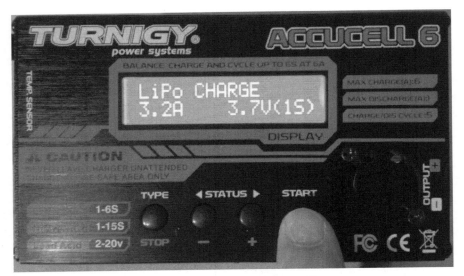

Typical Smart (Balancing) Battery Charger

PLEASE READ AND UNDERSTAND SAFETY CAUTIONS REGARDING LIPO BATTERIES - DO NOT CHARGE UNATTENDED AND CHARGE ONLY ON NON-COMBUSTIBLE SURFACES. See our Safety Appendix at the end of this book.

Wrapping it Up

We've covered most of the basics and even a little extra! The most important thing is to get yourself a quad (or a sim program) and start flying! Pay attention to the safety issues and use your common sense to avoid losing or destroying your drone during the first few flights. Keep at it and you will discover the joy of flying!

Some basic troubleshooting tips as well as a glossary follow. Keep this book handy and use it as you advance in the hobby. Also, be sure to visit our site at Droneflyers.com and sign up for our forums where experienced flyers can help you with your questions.

Thanks for Reading! Hope to see you at the web site and forum.

Craig Issod - http://droneflyers.com

Appendix
Safety Warnings and Topics

Please become familiar with the many safety issues which apply to this hobby. An outline of the major safety points is below:

Spinning Propellers can injure humans and animals - mid sized and larger quads could cause deep wounds or worse. Be cautious - do not fly near people and animals. Make certain you are familiar with the startup process (arming) of your quadcopters. Remover propellers when first testing new setups. Use a file or sandpaper to slightly dull the sharp edges of propellers.

Lipo Batteries can ignite as well as cause shocks. Do not charge batteries near combustible materials and do not charge unattended. Use special made LiPo batter charging sacks. Make certain there are smoke and CO detectors in the areas where you charge and store your batteries. Make certain that water and other fluids do not come into contact with your LiPo batteries. Make certain the wires and connectors cannot easily short circuit.

Falling or Crashing larger quadcopters can injure or even kill. As stated before, do not fly over or near people, animals or moving vehicles. Use common sense in planning your flight path.

Keep a small fire extinguisher in your flying kit - and in your hobby room. An ABC extinguisher should be fine for most secondary fires.

Do not use GPS when flying indoors - erratic results could result in lost control.

Troubleshooting your Quadcopter

Following is a list of common quadcopter malfunctions and their possible causes and solutions.

Problem: Quadcopter will not take off - props seem to spin at high speed but quad flips or just skids along the floor or ground.

Solution: Carefully check that all blades are installed properly - two types of blades are used on quads, clockwise and counter clockwise. Your owners manual should have a sketch of the proper layout - the higher edge of the blade should be leading the way!   The diagram below will pertain to many quads propeller rotation.

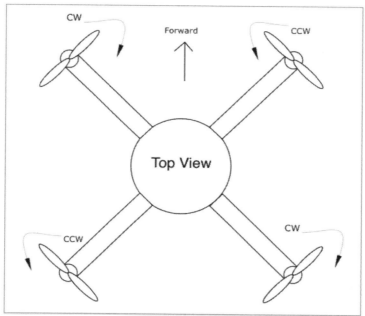

Problem: Quadcopter wobbles when hovering - even with light or no wind.

Solution: Carefully inspect propellers both while hovering (look at the pattern they create while spinning) and when the quad is off. Chances are that a propellers is out of shape from crashes or wear. Fix or replace.

Problem: One motor seems to take longer to start or spin up to speed.

Solution: This, in itself, may not be a problem as long as the quad acts correctly when more throttle is applied. It is somewhat normal for the props not to all start at the same instant. If, however, it affects liftoff or flight the motor (in minis and micros especially) may need to be replaced.

Problem: Quadcopter acts differently after 5+ minutes of flying.

Solution: Battery voltage may have dropped, resulting in different performance characteristics. Although flights can be as long as 10+ minutes, this depends on the battery size, number of cycles it's been through, charge state, etc.

A fresh battery should fix the problem. For larger quads, you should become familiar with the amount of voltage your quad needs to fly and use a digital multimeter to check voltage if you have concerns about a particular battery.

Problem: Quadcopter does not hover well, instead flying in one direction constantly.

Solution: As with many computerized systems, the first thing you should do is a reboot - accomplished by disconnection of the battery and reconnection, making 100% sure that the quadcopter is on a level surface. If your quad still favors one direction after a reboot, check the TX trim and adjust as needed.

Glossary

808 camera - A common name for a range of tiny "spy" cameras often sold as "Keychain" cameras. There are very light in weight and used by many hobbyists for taking video from multirotor and winged aircraft.

accelerometer - An electronic component which measures acceleration on a given axis (direction) of flight.

AP - Aerial Photography - a field which is growing fast due to smaller cameras and better aerial platforms

arduino - An open source (free software) project centered around a low cost circuit board which allows for control of objects. It is easily programmable allowing for experimentation. Many quadcopter control boards (FC, Flight Controllers) are built using this board and software.

ARF - Almost Ready to Fly - used to describe the Drone or Quadcopter you are purchasing - as to what it comes with! ARF units often come without the transmitter and may require some easy assembly

autonomous - not subject to control from outside, often used to describe a drone which follows a preset path using GPS or other means, as opposed to being actively steered by radio control.

axis - Used to describe one plane (one line) of potential flight. Most quads have at least 3-axis control and correction built in.

balancing battery charger - A charger or internal system for Lipo batteries (or other chemistries) which uses smart technology to properly charge multiple cells within the battery and "balance" them.

barometric pressure sensor - A device which uses barometer readings to determine altitude. In combination with other sensors, these can help drones determine their height above ground.

bind - The process of making the controller (Transmitter) "talk" to the Quadcopter or drone.

BNF - Bind N (and) Fly -This usually describes a unit which is ready to BIND to your existing transmitter and then fly.

brushless motor - Lightweight brushless motors are one of the defining features of the recent growth in popularity of electric aircraft. Brushless motors are categorically far more efficient, and far more durable than brushed motors. With small props, they can also be operated without the gearbox often required of lower RPM brushed motors, saving weight and wear on several fragile mechanical linkages. (dronepedia attribution)

build - Used an a noun when discussing home-built quadcopters or multirotors - example "Here's a picture of my build".

CA - Cyanoacrylate adhesive - also called superglue. This, along with Gorilla Glue and Liquid Tape, are often used in the building and repair of aerial vehicles.

camera gimbal - This describes a camera holder, often used on drones, which may have the capability to tilt and swerve using small actuators called servos. Various camera models, including video cameras and even large DSLRs, can be fitted to these gimbals.

center of gravity (CG) - Also called mass center - on a multirotor this is likely to be the point where, if a string were attached to and the machine dangled from it, that the unit would be balanced. It is important to maintain CG when adding different batteries, cameras, mounts, etc.

CF - Carbon Fiber - a very lightweight and strong materials used in aircraft and other items requiring a high strength to weight ratio

DJI - DJI Innovations, a highly regarded multirotor manufacturer who sells both kits, completed units and parts including the popular NAZA flight controller.

drone - A newer, perhaps slang, definition is for any unmanned powered aerial vehicle, although the dictionary has not yet caught up! In terms of the news and current events, it is often used to describe aerial vehicles which can be guided from afar and contain surveillance gear, etc. Officially, "drone" defines a humming sound or a male bee which mates with the queen.

dual rates / expo - often abbreviated as D/R, these are adjustments inside the hobbyist transmitters which allow for the user to "turn up" or "turn down" the way in which the aerial vehicle responds to the TX. The "dual rates" part allows for a TX to have two modes (i.e. easy and hard angles of flight) selectable by a switch. Expo or exponential sets the "curve" of the throttle and other controls.

ESC - Electronic Speed controller - this to used to speed up and slow down motor "RPM". These devices are the key to modern multicopters and most have one one wired to each motor.

flash - To reset and/or add computer code to a chip or controller.... i.e. "I flashed the ESC".

FPV - First Person View - often used to describe cameras mounted on aerial (or any unmanned) vehicles which let the operator see what the vehicle sees in real time. This is done by way of goggles or screens which display the output of the on-board cameras.

Gimbal - Mount for Camera which uses electronics to keep the camera level as your drone flies. This is accomplished through the use of 2 or 3 small motors which constantly adjust the leveling of the camera.

GoPro - A line of small lightweight sport cameras which are often flown on multirotors to capture video. They have a wide angle of view and are built to withstand shock.

GPS - Global Positioning System used to track movement or hold position on certain advanced Multirotor models.

gyro - Same as gyroscope

gyroscope - A device that measures angular velocity and helps maintain orientation.

hobby grade - describes a quadcopter or parts one step up from toy grade - these quads or parts are typically designed for better reliability and operation. Examples include quads such as the new RC Logger Extreme Eye One (brushless motors, etc.), the DJI Phantom, AR Drone and Blade 350X QX.

hexacopter - A multirotor aerial vehicle with 6 rotors

interval shooting - Settings which allow a camera to take pictures or video at user-defined intervals. Example: a camera can be set to take one picture every 5 seconds.

intervalometer - a software or hardware mechanism which allows interval shooting.

JST - A type of battery connector (plug) used on many quads. The other popular style is called the Walkera Connector. You can buy adapters which convert one to the other.

KAP - Kite Aerial Photography - taking pictures from a kite.

LIPO - Also called Lipo or lipo, etc. These are the type of battery (internal chemistry) that most electric drones currently use.

mAh - milliampere-hour - an electrical measurement of the power packed into a battery. One thousand mAhs equals one ampere hour. Quadcopter batteries will range in size from 50 mAh to 5000+ mAh.

mod - modification - quad and drone flyers love to modify their machines in various ways!

multicopter, multirotor - An aerial vehicle with multiple rotors (propellers which are horizontal). This would include tricopters, quadcopters, hexacopters, octocopters, etc.

multiwii - General purpose software initially developed to support Nintendo Wii console gyroscopes and accelerometers. It is now used to control multirotor aircraft. The software is now installed on many Arduino circuit boards, including custom models specifically for quadcopters.

NAZA - An electronic flight controller used on mid-level and above multirotors - produced by a company called DJI, The NAZA contains the main controlled chip along with a gyro, accelerometer, and a barometric altimeter. Optional GPS & Compass modules are available.

octocopter - An aerial vehicle with 8 rotors.

payload - The amount of weight your aerial vehicle may be able to lift in addition to itself and it's batteries.

pitch - used to describe the angle of flight along one axis - in the case of quadcopters, usually from level.

quadcopter - An aerial vehicle using 4 rotors, commonly using only the varying speed of the motors to achieve both stability and direction of flight.

R/C - Another way of writing RC - Radio Controlled.

RC - Radio Controlled - this refers to most multirotors and quadcopters which are controlled by radio transmitters or even by a smartphone or tablet.

RTF - Ready to Fly - In the field of Multirotors, quad (and other) copters and other R/C (radio controlled) vehicles, this means that the unit is sold complete with everything - ready to go. Note - you may still need regular (AA AAA) batteries for the transmitter)

rx - short for receiver or receive

servo - short for servomotor or servomechanism. On quadcopters and other aerial drones, these are used for various tasks (pan cameras, adjust wing flaps) and controlled by the radio from the ground.

telemetry - Refers to a back and forth connection between an aerial vehicle and your controller/transmitter/screens. This would allow, as an example, the display of the battery power remaining on the multirotor to be displayed to you at your ground station.

throttle - Control used to increase or decrease the RPM (speed) of the electric motors

toy grade - Describes many of the common quadcopters which cost less that $100 - these use very inexpensive components and are somewhat disposable. Reliability can be spotty, however they provide good value for the price.

trim - verb or noun describing the small adjustments on the TX to make a quad hover or fly correctly.

tx - Short for transmitter or transmit

UAV - Unmanned Aerial Vehicle (drone, etc.) or unmanned autonomous vehicle

ultrasonic sensor - A sensor which uses sound waves - in the case of quadcopters and multirotors they are usually used to determine the distance from the ground by bouncing sound waves off of it. In typical use, they work only for a few meters above the ground or other surface.

WOT - Wide Open Throttle - throttle stick on maximum!

yaw - used to describe the rotation of a quadcopter on a level plane around it's center axis.

Some Models for your consideration in 2014

* are suggested for beginners...

Under $100

*Blade Nano QX – Micro Quad with great features

*Hubsan X4 H107L – updated version of the most popular micro

*WL Toys v212/222 – Mini quadcopters with 6-axis stability – 222 is with camera, 212 without

WL Toys v262 – Larger version of a 212 series with decent payload capacity (see our review)

Under $200

Eye One Extreme – Brushless high quality quadcopter

Under $500

DJI Phantom (original model) has been on sale for approx. $400 - The new Phantom FC40 is now approx. $500 including FPV basic camera.

Blade 350 QX – Advanced Quadcopter with GPS, Altimeter and more.

Under $600

Walkera QR X350 GPS – Full size Quadcopter with GPS and other advanced features – large payload.

$900+-

3DR Iris – Advanced programmable expandable quadcopter from 3D Robotics

DJI Phantom Vision 2 and Vision 2+ - full featured photo and video platforms.

3D Robotics Iris

Links (mid-2104)

Informational Resources

Droneflyers Blog
http://www.droneflyers.com
Droneflyers Forum
http://www.droneflyers.com/talk

RC Groups Multirotor forums
http://www.rcgroups.com/aircraft-electric-multirotors-790/

DIY Drones
http://diydrones.com/

Tom's RC Pro Reviews - Lots of quad reviews and also TX setup guides
http://www.rcproreviews.com/

Hackmods - Lots of detailed stuff about modifications to quads and other R/C
http://www.hacksmods.com/

AR Drone Forums
http://www.ardrone-flyers.com/forum/
http://forum.parrot.com/ardrone/en/

FPV sites
http://www.fpvmanuals.com/
(Site with extensive documentation - also sells FPV systems and quads)
http://www.amazon.com/The-beginners-guide-Fpv-amp/dp/1300820004
(Book - Beginners Guide to FPV)

Shops and Products

Massive RC - USA vendor of micro and mini quads
http://www.massiverc.com/

Parrot AR Drone
http://ardrone2.parrot.com/

Banggood.com - Chinese vendor - low prices and decent reputation
http://www.banggood.com

List of Manufacturers -

Consumer (toy) and Hobby level multirotors

Note: This list is not complete - there are many companies entering and/or leaving the business. Also, many companies sell the same model(s) labeled with other brand names (private label)

Amax Toys
Arducopter
Ares RC
Armattan
Blade
DJI
Draganflyer
Dualsky
Estes
Eye One (RC Eye)
Foxtech
Gaui
Helimax
HJ Toys
Hobbylord (Bumblebee)
Hubsan/Traxxas
Idea-fly
Jdrones
JXD

MiKocopter
MJX
Parrot (AR Drone)
RClotus
Redcon
SH toys
Skyartec
Syma
UDI
Vitality
Walkera
Witespy
WL Toys
Woodon Toys
Xpro Heli

Made in the USA
San Bernardino, CA
23 June 2014